The D ͏ Yearbo

Modern Meditations of Inspiration

Sandy Wiseman

Fairmoon Limited
Nottingham

The Druid's Yearbook

Published in the UK by
Fairmoon Limited
9 Baker Rd, Giltbrook, Nottingham, NG16 2FZ

First edition 2001

Printed and bound in Great Britain by
Parchment (Oxford) Ltd

© Sandy Wiseman 2001
ISBN   0 9541772 0 7

Contents

To my family, to my awen-son, my husband, my steadfast gran, grandad and great-gran. And to Coifi and all those who ever encouraged me to find the magic within.

4

Foreword

Sitting up on the ridge, I watch the sun slide towards the mauve hills that are my far horizon, taking in with every breath the exquisite silence that he draws, like an ocean tide, behind him. Blinking slowly, my outbreath sinks gently into the earth beneath me. There is nothing to do, the moment filling every purpose within my soul. The scents of dusk glisten in the air.

The value of any spirituality, however clearly formed or vague, is in the pauses it encourages us to take. We are guided to stop and, calmly, to consider the purpose of our haste, the tangle of our priorities, the relevance and integrity of what we do. The power of Druidry in this respect is that its focus is not upon some world beyond life; instead it teaches us to see the beauty and sanctity that is the quintessence of the world within which we live.

As an ancient magical religion, its priests reached to the powers of nature, of fire, thunder, ocean waves, death, love and rage, seeking understanding, relationship, cooperation, in order to ease the uncertainty of life's tides. The foundation of the tradition remains the same; in the secular Western world, where too often people feel detached from nature, alone, losing a sense of life's purpose, those studying Druidry quest the inspiration that comes with pure connection. Finding relationship, spirit to spirit, we are infused with awen, the flowing spirit of creative energy.

Wherever we live, amidst the clamour and lines of the city, the colour and scents of the greenwood, there is exquisite value in pausing to perceive again the simplicity of the moment, to feel the calm that is presence, the gap between past and future. In these moments of meditation, we see again the beauty of nature, within us and around us. We learn to live with honour.

Beauty, serenity, inspiration
Emma Restall Orr (Bobcat)

Introduction to Meditations

To use these meditations, you need only a mind and your experience of life. You do not need to be a druid or know the reality of modern druidry, or to follow any religion. However, these meditations will especially help those following a druid path, or those who wish to follow the Druidic spirituality. They can take anything from 30 seconds to 30 minutes, depending on your need. You may find them helpful in the morning more than the evening, but try and find time between everyday matters. You will need to find secluded space, unless you don't mind your family witnessing you, for example, dancing the dance of bull-in-a-china-shop!

Meditation is relaxing and stress-relieving. There is certainly no need for awkward postures. You can meditate outside, standing at the banks of a river, sitting in a stone circle. Or inside, in a favourite chair, lying down, even in the bath.

There is no need to follow day one with day two; the commitment is on your own part, and no one will disapprove if you miss a day or a week.

Try not to dip into the book randomly, or look up family birthdays, searching for 'a good one'. The meditations are purposefully balanced between easy and hard, fun and intelligent, light and dark. You'll miss the point – without dark, what is light?

The meditations are a tool for you to use; flickering imagery based on simple themes. Some are pathworkings, other are simple phrases. All of them are beginnings, starting points, questions to begin your pondering train of thought that can last as long as you wish.

They are arranged seasonally in line with the Northern Hemisphere. If you are in the Southern Hemisphere, simply rotate the dates by six months.

How to meditate

Your meditations can last as long as you wish. Read the meditation through, maybe once or twice. Your mind will begin to associate ideas with the words, for example 'salmon' might make you think of a fish in your local supermarket or the splashing battle of a fisherman.

Allow your mind to follow a train of thought, a daydream maybe. If you find yourself going slightly off-track, then gently bring your mind back to the ideas you had. If you go off track more often, perhaps you need a more relaxing environment – candles, incense, a bath, anything that allows you to focus on the amazing store of information inside your head (and outside it!) will all help.

Let your meditation be active. Don't just sit back idly and watch the images wash through your head, ponder them, pursue them, and at times interact with them.

Whenever you can, try to go outdoors. Druids love the world and want to be part of it. Sitting in a beautiful natural place will be a good tool for you to use during your meditations to relax you. In addition, the spirits of the place may wish to help guide your thoughts, giving you the benefit of their ageless wisdom.

If you have been meditating for some while now, you may have made a connection with a particular helpful spirit (by spirit, I mean soul, being, person, ancestor, totem or familiar, not a ghost or anything difficult or spooky). By all means share your meditations with the helpful spirit, in order to receive extra guidance.

Druid tolerance and diversity precludes me from dictating to you how to meditate. There are many ways, and mine is not greater than yours. If it feels right, the result is inspiring, and no one is coming to harm, follow it and review it as changes come to your life.

Pre-meditation relaxation ritual.

Find yourself a comfortable space. Affirm to yourself why you are here – for example to spend 15 minutes meditating on the subject for today with the aim of knowing myself and the universe better and to connect deeper with my spirituality.

Breathe naturally. To relax more, focus on outward breaths through your mouth. By concentrating on the outward breath, the body responds by drawing in enough oxygen in the inward breath, without the need for concentration.

Imagine breathing out the unwanted carbon dioxide. Systematically relax your body.

My toes are relaxed
My fingers are relaxed
My feet are relaxed
My hands are relaxed
My ankles are relaxed
My wrists are relaxed
My calves are relaxed
My forearms are relaxed
My knees are relaxed
My elbows are relaxed
My thighs are relaxed
My upper arms are relaxed
My bottom and hips are relaxed
My shoulders are relaxed
My tummy is relaxed
My chest is relaxed
My neck is relaxed
My ears are relaxed
My face muscles are relaxed
My tongue is relaxed
My eyes are relaxed
My mind is relaxed

If you find it helpful, do this twice, once as preparation and the second time to complete the relaxation.

After the meditation, come back to the world in a similar gentle way.

If you are finding it difficult to feel relaxed, one way you can awaken your body to feeling relaxation is by taking a bath. Then, unplug and let the bath water out, whilst you are still in the bath. With each breath, your body will be less supported by the water, and feel heavier, so the water will help you understand relaxation as it runs out.

Consider your meditation throughout the day, as it is likely to be of great benefit to you. Meditating every day gives a perception of how everything is important.

You may also want to keep a diary of your experiences. It is very useful to re-read your path and encouraging to see how far you've come. When you don't feel like meditating, reading your diary can remind you how beneficial it is, and sometimes substitute.

Above all, relax, and be alert to the wonderful flow of inspiring Awen.

January

1 – You,
What do you look like from different perspectives? Try these perspectives: the carpet, an alien, your great great grandfather, the spirit of the apple sitting in your fruit bowl, inside out, the homeless man, the electricity cabling through your walls.

2 – Finding a space.
Seek out a space today, either physically or mentally, to call your own, to use for meditation. If you already have a space, reassess it, and maybe look for a new one.

3 – The Alder. (Fearn) Spiritual Guidance.
Blessed Alder tree,
Friend of water, element of spirit and intuition,
You whose sap bleeds when cut, we adore your humanity.
You faerie tree, who crosses the tides of this and the other world,
Be my bridge to the other bank-side.
Stretch out your arms that I may seek to enter the other realms and be guided in my path.
Blessed Alder tree.

4 – Treasure.
What are the treasures of Winter?

5 – Snowflakes.
Soft snowflake, falling gently, you disappear when you touch my palm. Let me meditate on your six turning arms, considering the turning of life. You are a reminder of childhood, and of age.

6 – Hearing.
Spirit of life, let me express my happy gratitude at the number of ways I can sense life around me. I am thankful for hearing, which sometimes stretches further than sight inthis age of enclosures.

7 – Sea
Pathworking: Be a fish or a mammal swimming in the ocean, beneath the turbulent wave peaks. What is it like?

8 – Man.
Meditation: Father Sun, Father Sky, Uncle Rain, Grandfather Frost. What else is Man?

9 – Woman.
Meditation: Sister Moon, Lady Ocean, Grandmother Hag, Earth Mother, Mother Nature. What else is Woman?

10 – Bull (Tarbh) Strength and potency.
Active meditation: Dance the part of Bull as you see him – stomp and snort, put your fingers for horns and chase shadows. Bellow. Be alive.

11 – Silence
Thought: Where can you find true silence?

12 – Druidry is an oral tradition.
To pin it down would be to let the point slip from your fingers. To write it down enslaves your children to your ideas.

13 – Feathers.
Pathworking: You hear a rustling from a tree near your favourite place. Looking up, you see a woman sitting in the tree, wearing a cloak of feathers. She grins and bellows. You climb. She invites you under her cloak to share her meditations. Afterwards, you thank her and leave.

14 – Smoke – Fire in the air.
Activity: Light a candle and watch not the flame. Watch the curls and ripples of the smoke. Just relax and watch.

15 – Salmon (Brionn Fhionn)
Salmon of the lake,
Salmon of the river,
Salmon of the Ocean,
I do you honour.
Most aged primal beast
Who dwells in the depths of forever
Eating the crisp hazelnuts
Of bittersweet wisdom,
I will swim with you,
Splashing in the wet.
Maybe I can absorb
Something of your magic.

16 – Communion
Activity: What are the dictionary definitions of communion and commune? How can you commune better with the land and world about you? Do you have opportunity to start today?

17 – Power of Nature
Once, the tallest object in the land was a tree, the brightest night-light the moon. The yule-dip of the sun was of enormous importance in an age without electric lighting or central heating. A druid who understood the turn of nature's cycle and phases of the moon would have been very much revered. Are you called to reignite the wonders of these mysteries or to help mankind process the new wonders of their world?

18 – Clouds
Meditate on the clouds, watch their forms and shapes. Do you recognise any shapes? What relationships are there between different clouds? How does wind effect them? Can you divine any meaning?

12

19 – Stonehenge
Meditation: Built 4,000 years ago (Trilithons), how much have the stones seen come and go? How important does that make us? It was built as a huge political or religious statement. What does this magnificent spirit say to you?

20 – Trees
Pathworking: A Derwydd (Welsh "Druid") stands in front of an oak tree, as if it were a person with who he was holding a conversation. There is silence. Finally he turns around, noting your presence, and greets you. Politely, you ask him what he is doing. He tells you "this tree is older than me, was asking his opinion on something." Confused, you enquire further. The Derwydd smiles and says "trees know much more than the books they are made into. Why don't you talk to him." He steps aside and you approach the oak. A sense of welcoming spirit reaches gently to you. Begin your communication. Afterwards, thank both Derwydd and oak, and return.

21 – Responsibility
A druid must be responsible for his or her actions: in spirit and body. Anyone who seeks knowledge and wisdom must be prepared to use it responsibly. In ancient times, a druid was so honoured that he could walk between battle lines to monger peace. His honour came through his responsibility to the greater good.

22 – The farmers of our food.
Pathworking: A homo sapiens, unable to follow his tribe with the migrating animal flocks, has stayed in his round tent-house with his heavily pregnant wife. Returning from hunting, he brings a gift of handfuls of seeds. His woman, thick with pregnant hormones is unable to receive his gift and shouts and snarls him away from her, tears and progesterone flowing. She knocks his hand, and the seeds fly scattered into the earth. He retreats, hurt, into the home, where a gathering of berries, meat and nuts is waiting. Her tears water the seeds, sown in emotion. Then she gains control

and returns to her husband, waiting confused and hungry. In the summer, their small daughter is born, and a scattering of beautiful sunflowers grace their new garden.

23 – Sky
Air above,
Speckled with stars,
Soft quilted bed
Where sleeps sun & moon.
How glad am I
That you swirl around my feet
So I can breathe!

24 – Gentleness
Pathworking: A woman Elder gives you a fragile forget-me-not. You hold it gingerly, afraid of breaking it. Then she leads to you a young lamb, gentle yet still lively. She takes your other hand and leads you to a willow giant. In the breeze the branches gentle tickle your face. At last she speaks to you: "Go gently. Your big boots may crush something important. Go gently, but don't let it hinder your liveliness. Go gently, and feel the joy."

25 – Druidry
Write down what druidry means to you. Don't share it, but keep it to reflect upon next year.

26 – Sight.
Blessed be the sense of sight, without which there would be no colour in this life. Blessed be sight, which brings us communication through actions and body language. Great spirit of god, I express my thanks for all I can see, look at, watch or spy.

27 – Bulb
A crocus, a daffodil or tulip am I?
I no longer know,
So deep was my sleep.
All I can feel is the lure of the sun,

Penetrating my shell,
Soaking within;
And the itch of growth
Like a stone in my shoe,
Sand in my socks,
Rubbing and begging for freedom –
My sprout!

28 – Spiral
A spiral turns inwards and it turns outwards. In wards it focuses, grounds and enthralls. Outwards, it is generous and flings power to the omniverse. Meditate on the curly spiral and use it for focus or control enthusiasm.

29 – The Dew of the Morning
Morning dew is blessed by the moon, and thought by some to grant beauty and longevity. Whatever the allegations, it is a wonderful morning wake-up wash, and imparts a gift of earth communion.

30 – Thought:
Will this cold ever end?

31 – Teenagers
Thought: Young man, young woman. You are so eager to burst from the bonds of safe childhood. Tomorrow's hope, today's despair! Join with us in honouring the ancient spirits. Your youth does not release you from humanity.

February
1 – Remembrance:
Our Misspent Youth. Are you perfectly happy with the way that you spent your youth? Take some time to linger on the way that children must learn and re-learn with each generation that passes. Imagine how hard it must be for a great grandma not to try and stretch out a hand to help.

2 – Imbolc, Feast of Brigid, Bride's Day, Candlemas.
Meditation: The preparation of the Bride, the maiden in her snow white gown.

3 – Beauty of the Spring.
Can you get outside to look around? It may be still cold or even snowy, but the light of Spring is beginning to show – snowdrops, longer daylight hours, ideas beginning to form in your head, itchiness to tidy the house. Get outdoors and rejoice at the potential that is growing and leaking from the sky and earth.

4 – The Willow.
Flexsome Willow,
Riverside dancer,
Perch of the cunning,
And friend of Alder.
Your long branch eyelashes
Dip in the lake of tears.
Teach us that weeping
Can be more than waterdrops.

5 – Moon
Consider the full moon on a clear night..

6 – The idea of Celts. I
Open a path in your mind to a green field, snow recently swept away, bright with the wet rain of spring. Standing there is the embodiment of all the Celtic ideas. He is a warrior prince with flame coloured hair and brightly dyed clothing. He beckons you to approach him and allows you to touch his sword, and heft his heavy shield. You thank you for sharing with you, and leave him a gift.

7 – Blood
You are a drop of blood, racing through a body. Let your mind race through that body, determining from internal organs, muscle tissues and tenderness of the heart what person that body belongs to. In the same way, we can understand the world outside us, yet never to perfection.

8 – Poem
The bard knows the power of rhyme, how it helps to commit to memory and express the music hidden in language. Even those not called to the bardic path can enjoy the ebb and flow of words. Today, write a short rhyme about something important. If you prefer, read it only to yourself.

9 – Far and Wide
Druidry is no longer confined to Britain or Europe. What might be the differences studying and practicing in America, Australasia, Africa? Our pleasant neutral hills and valleys are swapped for desert, heat, typhoon, earthquake and extremities in weather. Stories of Welsh or Irish legends must be difficult to relate to. What have we got left when we trim away the local accessories; what is the essence of druidry?

10 – The idea of Celts II
Returning the field where you met the Celtic warrior, this time you meet a Celtic Druid. Walking closer you see she is a woman. Perhaps she demands the name 'Druidess', perhaps not. This time, her countenance and clothing are subject to your meditation. Are they Greek or Roman, plaid or rags? What is your idea? Thank her for momentarily humouring your imagination. Release her image and let it leave, returning to the hidden truth. The idea of Celts is just an idea.

11 – Druidry is an aural tradition.
In listening, you honour the world, and open yourself to the whisper of Awen. Put time aside today to honour druidry, perhaps

by reading a book, perhaps by listening to the earth, perhaps through communication with your ancestors and descendents.

12 – The treasures of spring.
Action: List the treasures of spring, starting with flowers such as snowdrop, and finishing with the joy of seeing the melting snow.

13 – Consumerism
Anyone who buys something for personal use is labeled a consumer. Are you happy being primarily as a user, a devourer? Perhaps you can find a way to give back to this world, to even out the balance slightly.

14 – The lonely.
Pathworking: In an ancient Scottish meadow, you reach an inpenetrable fence. On the other side is a farm worker, alone, going about his chores with a heavy heart. The scene changes to an incontinent homeless man, living in squalor in London. He's drunk. He is avoided by all. Tears drip down his face as he pats a matted-hair mongrel. Another scene change: a dumpy 14 year old girl sat in a classroom full of bragging schoolgirls with their first valentines card. She refuses to cry.

15 – Grass
Meditate upon grass – green life that covers so many of our hills, yet is mostly unnoticed and trampled n. Consider other things in this world we take for granted, such as water, home comforts, our family's love, and street cleaners. Do you dare to kiss your lawn?

16 – Solitude
Pathworking: A solitary druid sits at the woodland's edge, watching her tribe's merry-making around a fire in the darkness. They are celebrating a seasonal festival – lunar or solar – with wine, meat and song. The druid was the one that pointed out the festival, explaining something previously frightening to them. Even so, now the merriment is underway, her quest for knowing has led her to the outskirts, to observe and take notes, to watch

the omens, and to be alone with familiar friends at the forest/meadow boundary.

17 – Heroes
Who is your special hero?
Do you have one, two or zero?
Superman or the Queen?
Getafix or fair Athene?
Is it perhaps your solar dad?
Do your friends think you quite mad?
A beautiful silvery birch tree?
My hero, I suspect, is me.

18 – Our people
Just as we are partnered with the land, so we should honour its people. What is the nature of the spirits of the people in the land where you live? How are their temperaments and beliefs shaped by their land? Spend time meditating on the people of the land and come to a gentler understanding of them and their leaders.

19 – Badger (Breach).
Ferocious dear badger, you teach me about tenacity and courage in the face of overwhelming odds. You teach me that life is stubborn in the face of adversity, and that brave steps and determination can protect the home or lead me down a wonderful new road. Remind me to walk my life full of spirit, and that the rewards will be the fullness of life.

20 – The Gods of our Ancestors.
What are the gods and goddesses of your ancestors? Who are the spirits of the locality? Do they include gods you find difficult to understand, such as the Christian God, Norse gods, unnamed gods? What is your call regarding their worship?

21 – Yew tree.
Associated with death most closely, Yew can also teach us about respect and honour we should give to age. Who do you know

that deserves this respect? What honour do you owe them because of their gift of teaching?

22 – A baby's laugh.
Have you ever heard the carefree laugh of a baby? Absolutely deliciously pure inspiration!

23 – Lunacy
Does the word lunacy come from La Lune, the moon? Are you ever moon-struck? Do you need the tiniest drop of madness to stay sane, to inspire your genius, to ponder the unthinkable?

24 – Leaf buds
The tree life-force bursting free!

25 – What is it all about?
Watching nature carry on as it has for countless years, is this the answer? Connecting to the fire of life beneath, is this the answer? Talking with the spirits around, is this the answer? Trekking to a sacred hill, is this the answer? Knowing you are a part? What is it all about?

26 – Prayer:
Grant O God thy protection,
And in protection, strength,
And in strength, understanding,
And in understanding, knowledge,
And in knowledge, the knowledge of justice,
And in the knowledge of justice, the love of it,
And in that love, the love of all existences,
 And in the love of all existences, the love of God,
God and all Goodness.

27 – Man
Activity: List, without a dictionary, words beginning with 'man'.

28 – Flying
Pathworking: You are a young bird, about to fly for the first time. You stand at the edge of the nest, looking down through the branches. You look up to the sky and the other trees nearby and faraway. Filling with longing, you jump from the branch, fluttering wildly. You plummet to the ground, flapping and flailing. Death races towards you. Somehow, you get all the muscles working intuitively together, and you fly gently to a nearby branch, just like mamma and dadda before you.

29
If it's a leap year, take the day off! With all these serious meditations to come, you're going to need it. And don't forget to leap!

March

1 – Mother
Mum, something bad happened and I couldn't cope. I'm so glad I could just excuse myself and run to you. Your arms around me, my head in on your soft breast. Modron, dearest, you help me to cope.

2 – Spring. A chant:
The itchy itchy itchy itchy feel of the Spring that's coming.
The juicy juicy juicy juicy taste of the bud that's sprouting.
The hurty hurty hurty hurty pain of the lamb that's birthing.
The lovely lovely lovely lovely smell of the grass that's growing.

3 – The Sacred Landscape.
Our distant ancestors painted and sculpted the land around with chalk figures, burial mounds, pagan hills and stone, wood and earth bank circles. Meditate on the messages they tried to leave their descendents, a message of unity with the land.

4 – Ash tree.
Meditate on the world tree, with its head in the clouds and feet underground.

5 – The Sacred Circle.
In your special space, purposefully walk the edge of a sacred circle (clockwise/deosil). As you walk, consider the spiral of the year, and the strength of the circle, a shape with only one 'side'. When you have finished your circle, sit inside the sacred area, and feel the protective atmosphere that arises from defining a special place. When you are finished, retrace your steps to close the circle. If you are proficient in casting circles, take this time to feel the differences in each of the four quarters, north, east, south and west. Take this time to return to the basics of enjoying the sacred circle.

6 – Raindrops.
Fat ones, thin ones,
Viscious ones, cuddly ones,
A sprinkling! A soaking!
A cycling! A catalyst of life!

7 – Acorns
Pathworking: You are an acorn, fallen from oak-mother, at the height of your juciness. Feel the despair and anxiety as you lay in leaf-mold. Then feel the soothing wash of life-giving rain, soaking into you and coaxing your spirit. Finally, allow yourself to feel the climax of bursting your shell, shoots aching through the moist, vital earth, and the feel the promise of treehood to come.

8 – Shame
What is the most shameful, most embarrassing thing you ever did? What did you learn from it? Are you still putting that lesson into practice?

9 – Thought:
What story must you tell?

10 – The mysterious differences between man and woman.

11 – Monsters.
Once, standing stones, lightning, disease and predators were monsters. Today's monsters are the bills, the central heating breaking down, the mother-in-law, the nuclear fall-out and the dirty syringe.

12 – Heather (Ur).
Imagine a hill or pair of hills, covered with soft Heather. She represents the feminine soft side of nature. With her permission, clamber her tummy or soft bosom. Maybe you will have the courage to playfully roll and tumble down the blossomy hillside?

13 –Wrinkles
Come to me, pretty wrinkles,
Grace my face.
I welcome you as a sign
Of maturity and wisdom.

Sweet rays of gentle sunshine
That pour from my eyes,
I am not afraid of you.
You bless me

14 – Strangers
The girl in the post office
Smiled at me today.
She was counting out foreign stamps,

And gazing through the glazing
To the sunshine that beckoned.
Your letter will arrive tomorrow,
Touch wood.
Her world is full of tomorrows,
She's dreaming and scheming
To reconnect with the land.
I wish her good luck.

15 – Awen
Death defying, mystifying, balm applying, I am flying!

16 – Hare
Pathworking: A dark night, lit by full moon and stars. A hare sits in a field, gazing upwards. You ask him what he sees. There is a silence whilst he looks up, then finally, he answers, still adoringly staring at the moon. He says "I see behind and before, but I can't take my eyes off the lady."

17 – Familiars or totems
Pathworking: You go to your special place, and there find those animals with whom you have a connection. Those you love. ake time to talk and share with them. Introduce them to one another.

18 – Rivers
Meditate on the spirit of the river, from the gurgling spring to wide mouth at the sea, ever renewing from several sources. Ever giving to the moody ocean. River is the key to the flow of nature in our land.

19 – Teardrops.
Can you remember the last time you cried – was it in joy, laughter, anger, fear or sadness? Were you moved to tears? Did you fight them? Begin to remember all the times you cried. As you look on from the outside, imagine yourself as a discarnate spirit, sharing the tears of laughter and kissing the tears of pain. Remember

that the next time you cry, a future you will be sharing this time with you. You won't be alone. Take comfort.

20 – Full to Bursting.
If you have the opportunity (or if not, imagine), spend a day unable to speak. Speech has been considered the 'seventh sense'. Feel the frustration of having information to give and be unable to repeat it. Can you understand the shamanic need to convey the thoughts of the spirits around us who have no voices? Can you understand the need of the bard to sing the song?

21 - Eostra, Alban Eilir.
For druids who are also Christians, Easter-tide is also the time of the death of Jesus. For pagan druids it is a pre-fertility festival of ovulation, and egg-laying. Continue with the meditation of yesterday, and meditate on the climax to fertility, to new life in Jesus and new life in May Day (Calen Mai) to come.

22 – Patience versus desire.
Thought: a small boy drooling over a biscuit tin, sitting on a high shelf. The clock ticks.

23 – Swan (Eala)
Pathworking: You visit a magical underground fairy grotto. There in the cave is a small lake. Upon the lake are seven beautiful swans, perfectly white. They are singing in human voices in perfect harmony. Their songs are sweet and rich, neither male nor female. You hide behind a pile of rocks in the grotto and listen enthralled. Hum the melody that they sing. When you finish your mediation, hum again the melody and take it with you throughout your day. Each time you hear the tune in your head, remember the beautiful swan songs.

24 – Dream the dream.
What is a dream that's never dreamt? Spend time day dreaming about your dream, perhaps working out solutions to obstacles, perhaps just enjoying the wishful thinking.

25 – Repair
Sixty years ago, the motto was 'make do and mend', rather than fast disposal. Reconsider how much you waste. Teach yourself to repair, reuse and share. Think of it as a spiritual discipline.

26 – Cat. Freedom.
Pathworking: Close your eyes. You are a cat. Are you a cat in ancient Egypt or a cat in contemporary Britain? What colour are you? Do you have a home? What are your characteristics? What do you like doing the most? Whatever you like doing, you also enjoy your freedom. You are not commanded. You choose where you go, where to sleep, which lap to sit in. You are free.

27 – The Bard's muse.
O fairest of fair, O Gogyrwen, personification of Awen, most inspiring beauty. Gazing at you fills me with sweet treasures of milk, dew and acorns. Honey-apple muse, never leave me small and alone.

28 – Hag
In a world that adores youth, Crone and Sage are a mystery to us. Undertake a pathworking of your own to meet a crone or sage, to uncover that mystery and to share with them.

29 – Birds.
Raise a hurrah
For the return of tiny wings:
Happy blackbird, curious pigeon,
Motorbiking starling, shy wren.
Friendly robin, chirpy chaffinch,
Two-a-penny sparrow.
Industrious woodpecker,
Cuckoo and swift.
Late in the day,
And the morning choir song
That sprinkles fairy dust on the sunrise.

30 – Interfaith

Pathworking: Return to a forest glen, and meet a spirit who represents another faith, eg: an angel, indian god, or budha spirit. You may feel angry or scared that this spirit has entered into your special place. However, you follow the celtic tradition of offering food and drink before business. Share food. As you share, the spirit confesses curiosity at your eating customs and habits. You explain. A conversation arises that compares cultures and religions in an open and generous manner. Neither of you ever get around to 'business'. Afterwards, say goodbye and thank each other respectfully. If you really enjoyed yourselves, arrange another meeting.

31 – Butterfly

Gentle-coloured butterfly
Fragile twitchy flyer
My spirit flitters with you
Low, around and higher.

Sunbeam chasing little one
Playing your carefree games
Magic-hued swooping kiss
Your wings scribe out my names.

April

1 – The phallus

Firstly, the phallus can undeniably be a source of amusement. This April Fool's Day, think of all the names for the phallus. Aren't they silly? Have a laugh, then move on. Secondly, give thanks for the phallus as a source of the DNA recipe, giving a sprinkling of biomatter that the mother stirs in her magic cauldron. Finally, meditate on the phallus as the source of man's power, the source of his tender masculinity, the driving force of passion and power. Men must learn to embrace and understand this amazing power, not deny it.

2 – Hawthorn (Hauthe). Guardian of sacred wells/springs.
Pathworking: You are a dusty, tired traveler, walking from winter to summer. At last, beside the road, you spy a lone group of hawthorn trees forming a natural hedge. Some have a few scraps of bright material tied to its thorny fingers. Curiosity brings you over. The hawthorns guard a sacred spring. You leave an offering for hawthorn and the spirits of the spring and drink thirstily.

3 – Crow (Badb).
Crow of conflict, crow of change,
Crow of ancient godesses strange,
Crow of death, crow of story,
Crow of wisdom, crow of glory,
Sister of raven, proud and aloof,
Help me to know you're a speaker of truth.

4 – The Harp.
Singer of sorrow, joy or sleep.

5 – Skyline.
O beautiful horizon, rippling with green hills and decorated with multi-textured forests! When I am in a city I see you eaten and bitten into, with huge unnatural bites. I pine for you, I long to witness your sky-caresses.

6 – Parents
Thought: Our parents are for good and bad. They gave us the gift of life. It's easy to look at great-great-aunts who had failings, and forgive them. What about parents?

7 – Your aura
Activity: During the day, ascertain what you can about your aura. Did you receive news that made you feel blue? Did you see red? Were you green with envy? Where s the limit of physical proximity, after which you feel uncomfortable?

8 – Panda
Panda may be extinct in 50 years. Panda is the symbol of land-belonging. Despite human efforts, Panda will not allow scientists to interfere in its natural home, and remains mysterious in the wild. Pandas in zoos pine for the land, starving and becoming infertile. What is your link to the land?

9 – The Holy Spirit,
The energy through which deity creates the universe, linked with healing and prophecy.

10 – The song of the sun.
Pathworking: The sun, rising on a warm Summer's morning. As it rises, it sings in a warm, vibrant voice, as if it were singing in the celestial bathroom shower. No-one else can hear the song, which floods outwards like sunrays. As the sun heads for midday, singing with joy, you imagine you see it wink at you. Then the song fades away, into the local morning birdsong.

11 – Promises
Modern descendent of honour
Gate to the garden of trust
Rosebush of thorns and blooms
Keep a promise you must.

12 – The mysterious chemicals in our bodies.
Ponder the number of hormones, liquids and semi-solids in your body. You already understand blood, bones, skin, testosterone and oestrogen. What else is inside? The human body is amazing – a complicated, delicate, vital piece of art.

13 – Monks and nuns,
And all those equally dedicated to seeking god.

14 – Dance
Activity: In this staid and upright community, when did you last seen dance? When did the spirits around you last see dance?

Dance for them. It needs no special rhythm or grace, just willingness and laughter. If you're lucky, they may join in.

15 – Touch

Meditate on the sense of touch, associated with skin. A touch can be given or taken. Sometimes it only requires the touch of the wind on the hairs. A touch can heal, a touch can inform. Druids have been scorned as tree-huggers, but t is that which drives them to communicate to nature by touch and other senses which sets them apart.

16 – Blackthorn (Straif). Sticking our head in the ground.

Pathworking: A pub or meeting place in southern Britain. You sit with three friends. After general conversation, you turn the topic to housing that is being planned for ancient woodland. "Pete," you address the first. "You work in the council. Have you seen the plans for this development?" "Nope," he says. "I ain't seen nothing." He turns his attention away. You don't believe him. "Angela, you're Pete's secretary. Have you heard any meetings or rumours?" "I haven't really heard anything, no," she says. "John, you're the office junior. What do you think?" "Well…" he considers. "I might have seen something. I might not have. It's not really for me to say, is it? Can I get you another drink?" Hmm, you think. A right trio of wise monkeys! Does the development get built?

17 – Garden

Pathworking: Step from your special place towards a gate that leads to your dream garden. Your garden can be as large as you wish – a cliff or seashore or a more traditional garden, with lawn patch and shrubery. Is it formal and paved, or wild and overgrown? What flora and fauna exist there? Trees and deer, herbs and hawks or cactus and reptile? What does it mean? Do the flowers have great importance to you, or is solitude and north-wind that you desire? There is no rush to over-analyse. You can always come back.

18 – Your land
Activity: explore the history of your land and customs of your people.   Knowing your roots makes your branches stronger and fruit greater.

19 – Astronomy
How differently would Earth's spiritualities have developed if the universe had given us two moons instead of one?

20 – Horse riding
Meditate on a land and a time when there were no cars to overheat or breakdown in a flood.   Your transport had feet and feelings, and was once born to a mother that nuzzled and licked it dry.   Consider the other differences between car, cart, and horse.

21 – Mum-healing
Ponder this made up word that describes the basics of first aid intuitive to mothers and ovates with deep earth connections. Mum-healing takes place when a mother rocks her baby to sleep, when a father kisses his son's tears away, when a girl strokes a grandmother' cut with soothing words, when a sham sits and holds hands with the patient, listening.

22 – Orderliness
Druid groups are often organised into 'orders'.   Ancient druid teaching included the composition of poetry according to rigorous rules of alliteration and rhyme, and yet still expressing the beauty or truth of their subject.   Strict discipline thus ironically became the base of emotion wrenching verse.

23 – Lynx.
Pathworking: A wildcat, wandering over rocky ground dotted with trees and shrubs. It is able to pick the safest, quickest and most efficient way over the ground, intuitively knowing where to place its furry feet, sniffing the air and scanning the horizon with its

golden eyes. You sense it is not wandering at all, and quite purposeful, following a path of intuition. Where is it going?

24 – Poetry.
Have you ever felt a burden to express yourself beyond conversation?

25 – Thought:
"Burst forth in song"

26 – Wave
So much is conveyed in waves – the oceans, light, and female emotions and hormones. As in the natural circle of life, highs and lows are natural and undeniable. There are a myriad of ways to honour the waves of life during your day. Choose one.

27 – Taste
Active meditation: gather around you a little of every type of taste you can think of – sugar, lemon juice, ice, hot bread, metal, onions etc. Taste each one as a spiritual experience, as I it were a first communion. Meditate on your reactions.

28 – Future
How will following Druid meditations aid you in your future spiritual quest? Are you home now forever? Is it a step in searching? Will you ever get where you're going? Will you stay with Druidry, redecorating your spiritual home with personal changes, or must you move house eventually?

29 – A prayer
My dear gods, how happy am I that you are with me and care share my ecstasy and spirit-freedom that comes when I touch the awen and use myself to reflect that golden spark for use in healing or divining. For the days when waking is hard and I need the promise of awen. For the times I can connect with the spirits in the land, and see life from their perspective. Thanks for listening.

30 – Lust
Pathworking: You've been working hard in the field with your community. At sundown, you down tools and gather in the village hall.   There is food, drink and song.   A group of musicians start playing and dancing begins. A member of the attractive sex catches your attention, as they dance with their friends. They look totally different to when you worked in the fields with them earlier. Their skin sparkles, their eyes laugh and they are full of energy and happiness. They catch your eye for a second and dance on, flirting with their companions, yet their eye always coming back to tease with you.   Let the knowledge build up inside you, that despite the number of people dancing with them, it's you that they really want.

May

1 – Beltaine, May day, May feast, Calan Mai
Half-way through the Celtic year, Beltane is a celebration of the climax of love and union. Also the day the magical Tuatha de Danaan arrived in Ireland. A day to celebrate the maypole, morning dew and spring blossoms.

2 – Love.
Love, sweet love,
Overpowering and simple
All consuming and complex.
Your hand is upon me,
And my eyes open in joy.
I widen my nostrils
To breathe your perfume.
Enduring and fickle.
You will be my master
And I will be your hound.

3 – The discovery of Awen

I searched in my soul
And throughout the world,
For the spirit that guides me
Inspires and tempts on.
I glimpsed you at the stones,
With the peep-o of King Sol.
I smelt you in the grass dew
That the moon shone upon.

The fox and the rabbit
Left your whisper for their trail
And my true love left your tickle
In the touch of a hand.
I spied you in the lightning
And the deluge on the hills
You were in the giggle of the pixie girl
Who hid in the fog.

Can I never catch you?
Will you never keep still?
O lead on, honey spirit wind
In your game of kiss chase.

4 – Wedding

Pathworking: You are a guest at the wedding of a god and goddess – representatives of all that is male and female. Shut out the shouts of culture that demand to be heard, whether traditional, religious or national, and focus on the light at the core of the ritual. Is it the symbolic hand-holding, or the kiss, or the exchange of vows and contract? Seek out the core. If you find it, indulge by then sprinkling with pleasing customs and culture, eg supply a broom to be jumped, or a chalice to drink from. Celebrate.

5 – The Lady of the stars.
Pathworking:
Leaning back on a grassy hillock, you survey the night sky. The stars sparkle like gemstones being turning in the light. One twinkle grows larger and closer and you observe it is a chariot pulled by a silver horse. A woman guides the chariot and the turning of its wheels sprinkle flashes of light. She gallops closer. Not wanting to miss her before she rides off, you stand, and catch her eyes. She speaks a single, secret blessing-word to you, and journeys on, to disappear in a glitter of stars.

6 – Blaze
Sacred dancing fire
Or purifying smoke.
Let your flames burn higher
And light up all my hopes.

Saining and crackling,
Burning Winter's taste
Greedily licking brightly
And eating with haste.

Swallow my Winter
And present it to the air
As I too tread higher
On my circular life stair.

7 – Snake (Nadredd).
Pathworking: a brown scaled snake is coiling around the bottom of a flaky silver birch tree trunk. Fascinated, you watch as it winds its way back and forth, its skin loosens and the snake curls out. This time, it is a shimmering peacock colour. What is snake telling you about renewal?

8 – Yearning and wishing.
Meditate on the differences between yearning and wishing for something.

9 – Your relationship with nature
For your meditation today, go for a walk and appreciate nature around you. Separate yourself from the bustle of everyday life. With permission, find some new item for your altar at home, some new secret communion to cherish.

10 – Journey
In your pathworking today, journey temporarily outside your own culture. Visit a time and place you have never seen before, or maybe never even heard about. Feel your spirit friends go with you, to communicate with local spirits when it is beyond you. Feel your curiosity, and remember the universal tools of politeness and smiling.

11 – Future
Druid belief in reincarnation is not fixed or required, yet is still held by many. Supposing that time is linear, imagine the future, and the skills you might need, for example flexibility, imagination and determination.

12 – Clan
Light a candle and pray for and seek knowledge to enable you to better communicate your druidic experiences, such as the burst of Awen, to those you hold dear and those you share your life with.

13 – Beauty
Thought: Beauty is a gift given by yourself when witnessing in the light of Awen. Today, seek that flowing spirit to illuminate your innards and sparkle like light through eye-windows, bejewelling and giving the gift of beauty.

14 – "The Lord God will give me the sweet awen as from the cauldron of Ceridwen."
Acknowledge that inspiration comes from many sources, and meditate on these sources.

15 – Oak
Locate an oak and introduce yourself. (If you can't find one near you, turn this activity into a pathworking.) Get to know each other, you telling him what it is like to walk, he teling you about putting one's feet into soil. Touch each other and feel your differences in skin and sense what is underneath. What else do you talk about?

16 – Pagan dislike of Christians
Why have Pagans disliked Christians in the past? Why do they dislike them now?

17 – The Government
Compared to many people, we are lucky to have a government like the one we have. A druid belongs to the people, as does a government. Consider the historical changes to both and the changing fortunes of politics.

18 – Dusk
Ponder the magic of dusk – the time that lures out hidden animals. What is hidden inside you?

19 – Dawn
Meditate on the time of dawn. At this time of year, it brings warmth, light and joyous birdsong.

20 – Pain
Thought: without pain, illness and wounds would ravage our bodies untended.

21 – Climbing trees
A great way to gain a new perspective.

22 – The sunrise
More intimate than a sunset, sunrise brings a new day.

23 – Hound (Cu)
Pathworking: A hunter from ancient times lies on the grass, winded from a horse-fall. His hound stands over him, tail wagging, licking his face. The horse grazes peacefully, no-one else is around. The hunter laughs, then forgets his chase in the joy of communing with his dog. He rubs his ears and speaks lovingly to his devoted friend.

24 – Ethics
Can religion and ethics sit together?

25 – Spirits
What spirits reside near you that you do not acknowledge? The suspicious concrete spirit of the motorway? The plaintiff eager child spirit of the teddy bear? The unheard hush of the fallen catkin? The purple monster under the bed? Listen!

26 – Power
Is your god or goddess the most powerful thing in your life?

27 – Draw a tree
Firstly ignore any feelings of lack of artistic ability. Secondly don't draw a flat tree like a picture postcard, lie with your head in its roots and look up to its crown. Now draw a tree.

28 – Eagle.
Eagle, Eagle, King of the air. Lofty above me, you spy all. A mountain perch for a throne, wingspan for a robe. Your eyes take in all knowledge and hide it behind the cruel beak of experience. Totem of the wild knowledge-seeker and unattainable by most, I know you are just beyond the next mountain.

29 – The stars
Twinkle twinkle, little star,
How I wonder what you are.
Up above the world so high,
Like a diamond in the sky.
Twinkle, twinkle, little star,
How I wonder what you are.

30 – The British Horse
Sat on the Gorsedd Arberth mound, Prince Pwyll of Dyfed first glimpsed Rhiannon, Goddess of horses, also linked to Epona and the white chalk horses of Britain.

31 – Cauldron of Rebirth
Druidry does not demand a symbolic death and rebirth. The cauldron instead holds a life giving broth.

June

1 – Hot blood
To some it signifies impetuous adolescence, to others it is a sign of compassion and liveliness. Which is it to you?

2 – Locality
Druidry is not airy fairy or scholarly. It starts at home. Today, be on the lookout for local animals, and identify local plants. Build a picture of your locality

3 – Thought
Today is the first day in the rest of your life.

4 – Holly bush (Tinne).
Pathworking: Deep in the forest, there is a creature, half holly-tree, half man. You peep at him from behind a bush or tree. Around him are happy young animals, playing together. He spreads his outrageous branch-arms and addresses the tree-tops

with song: "O Summer, come, come to me the Holly King, o warmth come witness our joy! O Summer, come! I call to you!"

5 – Nemetonae –
Sacred enclosures and woodland sites in particular.

6 – The power of music

7 – Live the song!
What would your life be like if you lived like a character in a song? More colourful, more inspiring, more courageous, more caring? What song do you want to live? What song do you currently live. Meditate on the answers.

8 – Childwealth.
Meditation: The unlimited potential in new born life, the gifts of joy and wisdom children bring. No wealth can compare to the soulwealth children give freely to those around them.

9 – Lakes
Take an inner journey to a lakeside, sit and ponder its symbolism – stillness, the womb, abundance, the element of water.

10 – Three
A sacred Celtic number. The Celts had a triple goddess before a trinity. Other teachings also come in threes. Ponder triplicity.

11 – Cow.
Pathworking: You enter a peaceful Welsh village or settlement. Children play happily in the street. You look especially at one place, where a woman is milking a lowing cow. Her bucket is nearly full. A child stands by, stifling giggles as the father creeps up behind the woman then surprises her. Before the laughing subsides, he has taken her indoors to love. The perplexed cow is milked instead by the child. Cow represents harmony at home.

12 – Mother
Our birth-giver and first true love.

13 – Thought
Telegraph poles were once trees. Now they unite the land in communication.

14 – Ritual
Ritual creates communion and homeliness, familiarity. What are your familiar rituals?

15 – Saying:
If you go into the forest for a day, take bread for a week.

16 – Rest
As the heat of the sun approaches, take time to rest your body and spirit.

17 – Mouse
Pathworking: Returning to your sacred place of safety, you meet a family of mice. They are young, old, fat, thin, male and female. They all begin speaking and squeaking at once. You raise a hand for peace. Then they tell you their stories and you sit on the floor with them, listening. Some are stories of cheese-stealing bravery, others are ancient tales of decimation by humans. Listen to their stories, then tell them your story, translated for their easy understanding.

18 – Elder tree (Ruis).
I see you dryad!
Peeking out of the Elder tree
Spirit of bark and leaf
Old man, little girl.
Keeper of grainy wisdom
Buried deep in the wood.
Dare I embrace you
And hear your heartbeat?

19 – The Sun.
Loved and loathed alternately throughout the year, the sun is more than a type of weather – it is the cause of the seasons and the power behind life in this solar system.

20 – Fullness
Do not deny yourself the fullness of the experience of your life – seize the day and honour yourself with the gift of fullness.

21 – Midsummer, Alban Hefin
Some spiritual paths, such as Wicca, create a connectedness between priest or priestess and the full moon. In this meditation, connect with the Sun at its full strength. You may feel awe at the power, or gentle comforting warmth. Do you know any stories about how the sun rides across the sky? Do you know any myths about solar eclipses? Think about what the sun means to you in its greatest height.

22 – Community
Meditated on the death of local community and village support.

23 – Fighting within communities
Make a list of those who you don't get on with, such as those in your tradition who have different opinions. Also remember tensions in your family or at work. No-one will see the list, so don't worry about being honest. Petition yourself, your deities and your supportive ancestors, requesting help from inside and out, to bring peace into the relationships. You may wish to shred or burn the list afterwards, or to keep it as a lesson.

24 – The World
Meditate on the turning of the Earth, and its variety of seas and lands. Imagine or look at a real globe / atlas. What do you feel?

25 – Magpie.
Is everything black and white? If you look closely, Magpies are also bluey green. Meditate on the colours of the Magpie.

26 – The Land
Today, meditate deeply, taking your thoughts from your body, through your feet and deep into the land beneath. You may connect with the Spirit of the Land, or just the Spirit of the land beneath your feet. You may find yourself thinking about your country on a large scale, or find inspiration in spirits of earthworms, moles and land indwellers. With a deep meditation, be gentle with your return.

27 – Your altar
You have set aside daily time for yourself. If this is helpful to you, it's likely that it will be just as helpful to set aside special physical space. Create a small altar on a table or mantlepiece. Add photos, candles, statues, gifts from nature. You may be surprised that as you care for your special place, you care for yourself more, too.

28 – The Hearth.
Pathworking: A pre 20th Century family are seated round a low-burning hearthfire. You are a member of the family. The whole family are tired after a long day, and full of food cooked on the hearth. There is silence, apart from the crackle of low burning embers and human squirming as your family find more comfortable seating. The spirit of hearth stretches and relaxes, in perfect communication.

29 – Summer
What are the treasures of Summer?

30 – Cultural changes
In your culture, you might draw a line at dying your pet's ears and tail with the latest fashion, or at divination with entrails. What part of modern culture would your ancestors find difficult?

July

1 – Fire
Fire is a two sided coin. Warmth, light, growth – these are contradicted by burning pain, deserts, and destructive flames.

2 – Hazel.
The origin of wisdom. What gives you wisdom?

3 – Challenge:
Can you eat happily without cooking today?

4 – Exotic animals.
Action: Go to the library and take out a book (try the children's section) on exotic animals. Take it home, study it, and then laugh at the amazing differences between life on this planet.

5 – Doorways
There are many doorways in druidry – the doorways between light and dark at the equinoxes, the doorways of rites of passage, the shamanic doorways to the otherworlds, and the physical doorways at Stonehenge. Which are important to you?

6 – Ethics
Truth, justice, honour – which ethics do you hold to? Which are the most important, which are lacking today, and which are over-valued?

7 – Reincarnation
The belief that a spirit can live many lives, especially applied to humans. Initially taught by the Druids, and brought back to these Islands by Eastern Teachers. Is it a part of your belief?

8 – The three awens
Meditate today by chanting Awen (A-oo-wen) three times, listening to the resonance in your head and feeling the flood of coloured wind and smoke, curling and snaking around you. As it

curls around you, feel how much more luminous the world looks, and listen to the whisper of divine inspiration.

9 – Thought:
Some British longbarrows are older than the pyramids.

10 – The gentle all-father
Meditate on the masculine aspect of deity, but especially on the gentle all-father, omnipotent but lovingly paternal. What are your thoughts on him? Is he easy to contemplate?

11 – Peacock. (Paun)
Self-esteem meditation: Just for five minutes, imagine that you are six inches taller, and that you have the most beautiful blue, purple and forest green tail (perhaps peacock-shaped). Strut around and feel the spirit of the peacock rising within you. Do not be afraid – you are the most beautiful creature in the world. There is no-one to see you save those you invite. Meditate on the feelings that you receive.

12 – Lavender
Tiny lavender flower, full of amethyst juice. Your pure sweet smell will always endure, under the crushing intoxication of summer's burgundy blooms. Teach me the humility of tinyness, teach me the eternity of gentleness.

13 – Gardens
A refuge from urban bustle. A place of peace, where spirit can be honoured.

14 – Our food
Is it true: "we are what we eat"? What would you be? Do you care enough or too much about what you put into your body?

15 – Age
Age is inescapable. You can't stay a child forever. Take a piece of paper, write your age on it and decorate the paper. Celebrate! Today can be your secret "birthday" – your AgeDay!

16 – Aspen (Eadha).
In honour of Aspen, meditate on friendships. Consider your friends, a great gift, and the give and take friendship requires.

17 – Rest
Activity: compose a lullaby for yourself or someone you love.

18 – Humility
It is better to take the lowest place and be called to a higher table than to seat yourself at the head and be asked to step aside.

19 – Active meditation: Mini Hike
Take a length of string, rope or ribbon about 3 foot long, and lie it on the earth. Hike and explore along its path, inch by inch.

20 – The Four Directions

I call to the spirits of the East where truth and knowledge come from.
I call to the spirits of the South where the battle is fought and won.
I call to the spirits of the West where wisdom and honour are shared.
I call to the spirits of the North for the end and beginning is there.

© Carwgwyn, used with permission

21 – Misunderstandings
Meditational question: Which misunderstandings have happened to you recently? How have you been able to resolve them in peace?

22 – Strings
Meditational question: Is it a coincidence that the emotional moments are said to pull at the heart "strings", or is it a reference to the Bard's tools?

23 – Fox
Fox, I honour you for your cunning and your intelligent wit.
I thank you for the inspiration you give me when you make fools of your hunters.

24 – Thought:
What is most precious to you?

25 – Sunshine in the branches
Blessed are the leaves that filter the sunshine into marvelous floor dapplings. Wonderful is the game the sun plays with the tree tops, glinting, sparkling, and hiding like a coy lover playing May games.

26 – British Minerals
Part of the land of Britain, Wales is famous for gold, Cornwall for tin, Dover for its white cliffs. What minerals are there in your locality?

27 – The Summerlands
Challenge: what is your idea of the afterlife, of the Summerlands. Is your vision that of a Christian heaven, or the Pagan Western Isles? Does the idea of the Summerlands affect your beliefs in reincarnation or are your two opinions separate? Are the Summerlands a state of mind or a real place?

28 – Ovate
A diviner of nature, from the linguistic root 'uat' – to be inspired or possessed. Inspiration and possession by Awen being the basis of an Ovate's work.

29 – Forest Fire
Pathworking: You are a deer, or a fox, or a rabbit, or any forest creature of earth or sky. Feel the force and fear of the roaring forest fire approaching. Feel the exhilaration in terror as you bound through the undergrowth, heading over the river to sanctuary. Hear the crackle and taste the bitter smoke. Praise your god or goddesses for the ferocity of the renewal by fire.

30 – The flight of birds
Ovates once divined by the flight of birds. Today, little remains of the knowledge. Try mapping out the sky to represent questions, and using intuition divine answers according to which birds fly in which manner through which sky sections.

31 – Pruning
Consider human and natural pruning, and how it frees resources from the plant/tree. Ponder the spiritual aspects of pruning.

August

1 – First Harvest, Lammas, Lughnasadh, August Feast
Thought - the light at the end of the tunnel.

2 – Mulching and composting
Composting teaches us to care for the environment and to re-use our waste. Can you find a positive re-use for your emotional rubbish?

3 – Apple tree (Quert).
The three drops of liquid in Ceridwen's cauldron. The isle of apples. The pentagram hidden inside. Apple juice flows as you bite, like Awen. Sometimes it dribbles down your chin, but even that is nice.

4 – A rose
Often associated with aging aunts, the scent of a rose is delicate and sweet as a maiden. Together with the bloom and the thorns, a rose is a good representation of the Goddess.

5 – Quest
Inside a mythic cave, you find a group of dark age warriors and their king, asleep. In his right hand is a legendary sword, in the other hand is clutched a jewelled goblet. A dark-clothed man is guarding the company. He is seated by the fire, where a cauldron bubbles tonight's meal. "Ah, come in," he invites, grinning toothily. "Are you on a quest too?"
Speak with Merlin – give answers regarding your quest, and request help if you wish.

6 – Worm.
Thought: Stay grounded.

7 – Welcoming strangers.
Consider the difficult and noble task and how much it features in your life.

8 – Thought:
O god of my ancestors, older than oak, wiser than salmon, sweeter than honey, stronger than bear, guide me today.

9 – Smile at a stranger.
It won't hurt you, and it might even make you both a little bit happier.

10 – Concentration:
Allow a daydream to form and follow it. When you are ready, seize an image from the train of thought and turn it over in your mind. When the struggle is too much, release it. Repeat the exercise as you will – muscles grow through repeated use, not through straining past the limit.

11 – Grain
Meditate on the potential within a grain, and how much a grain can grow, like a little sun nuclear reactor.

12 – Imagination
Meditate on imagination as the sacred source of inspiration. How have you trained your imagination.

13 – Otter (Balgair).
Pathworking – you walk down to the edge of a stream or river. A perky otter runs up to you, coat glistening with water. You follow it back into the stream and splash along the banks after your frisky friend. The otter leads you to an area of the bank where a tree stands, its roots curving in and out the soil. Beneath the tree roots, the otter has hidden a hoard of silver, gold and precious jems, sparkling in the sunlight. The otter says to you that you too have hidden inner treasures.

14 – Diplomacy
Pathworking: two kings or politicians are seated opposite, followers nearby. Their arms are folded in stubbornness and resentment. A druid sits at the same table. He or she takes advantage of the silence to let slip silver words of diplomacy and power. With flatter, friendliness and straight presentations of the facts, the words work their magic. An apprentice druid stands behind, amazed, drinking in the relaxing of kingly tempers. The kings, smiling, turn the facts over between them, working together to solve their differences, the druid forgotten in the heat of co-operation.

15 – The cups of the body.
I pray that as Awen light shines on me, my base-cup of body is renewed and healed. That my belly-cup of mind overflows with inspiration. That my head-cup of Spirit be turned up to receive divine knowledge and understanding.

16 – Hands
Isn't it amazing that such strange lumps of flesh can create delicate art, poetry and music.

17 – Vine (Muin).
Relaxation – Inspired by the spirit of vine, today spend your meditational time relaxing.

18 – Suffering
Thought: In the time of greatest suffering comes the greatest overcoming!

19 – Wolf.
Now is the time to seek your own wisdom within. Other people can only give you a seed of knowledge. It is up to you to nurture the seed and pursue wisdom with ferocity.

20 – Dragon
Symbol of the earth's inner fire energy.

21 – Truth
Meditation on the endless quest for truth.

22 – Teachers
Active meditation: Make a list of your teachers, whether they know it or not. Write your own name at the top. Here is an example of the beginnings of my list: Me, Amairgin, Brigid, Emma, Anna, Caitlin, Mabel, Jamie, Hermis, Faichre, Bear, Margaret.

23 – Inspiration
Active meditation: Write a list of everything that inspires you and that which takes your inspiration away.

24 – Heat.
Remember yuletide, when you longed for every extra minute of light and warmth. Despite any heat discomfort now, give thanks.

25 – War.
Consider the changes in war methods over the last few thousand years. Compare the superstitious clan wars to today's remote control murder. What is the difference between yesterday's rape and village burning and today's nuclear or biological civilian killings? Allow your mind to skim over the whole concept of war. Find our how to donate something to charity for war victims.

26 – Places
Which place inspires you the most? Your garden, a riverside, the beach, a hilltop, a stone circle maybe? Meditate on inspiration given by places.

27 – Furze (Ohn). Barriers
Pathworking: You clear a path in your mind. At the end is a prickly hedge barrier. Drawing your sword, you chop through. You don't succeed, and tire yourself. This time, you give up, retreating to find another path. As you leave, the hedge closes behind you and you wonder if maybe it's a protection against something that ought not yet be disturbed.

28 – Raven (Bran)
Pathworking: before an ancient battle, you watch from a hill. The enemies are waiting, stirring themselves with song and drink. The ravens are circling. Some have settled near you, watching, waiting for the end of the crisis. The air is full of electricity. Even the earth beneath seems to be awaiting the blood that will be poured and the paid that will come and then fade.

29 – Green meadows
Meditate on the tranquility of meadows. Think about the plant life swaying, growing and blooming. Consider the birds and their songs. Ponder the invisible world of the insects, the busy ants, the grasshoppers and beetles.

30 – The spirit(s) of your home.
What spirits are there in your home? Naughty pixies, curious gnomes? Spirits of rest in the bedroom, spirit of heart in the kitchen?

31 – The oath of peace
"We swear by peace and love to stand, heart to heart and hand in hand. Mark, O spirit, and hear us now, confirming this, our sacred vow."

September

1 – Tradition
In Britain, September now marks a return to road congestion as parents drive their children to school, instead of walking as traditional. What other traditions have been lost recently?

2 – Wind
Watch the wind moving in the branches of a tree. Imagine it to be non translucent – maybe blue silk ribbons or bouncing oxygen atoms. Finally, watch the wind instead of the branch. Smile yourself an inner smile. You may find yourself repeating this during the day!

3 – Stag.
Hail master Stag, with your strong thick coat. I see you wear a regal crown high upon your brow. Lord of wildness, gentle and raging; your robe is made of steadfastness. Thank you for your lessons.

4 – Children's stories
What fairy tales do you remember from your childhood? Do any of them have lessons applicable to your adulthood?

5 – Your year
Active meditation: Divide a sheet of paper into 12, labelling each section with a month. Fill in important dates, such as the eight season festivals (sabbats/fire festivals), birthdays, anniversaries, nature changes, memories of holidays, etc. Meditate on the whole year, and its changing colours and flavours.

6 – Learning
It is better to question answers than to answer questions.

7 – Child
The cub, the kit, the lamb, the pup, that spirit that comes to you when you are trying to focus seriously, and says: "run with me! Play with me. Let's bite and lick and jump and learn. Come on!"

8 – Inspiration
Meditative questions: What inspires you to be creative? What makes you want to succeed in your daily work? What makes you bother?

9 – Support
Meditative questions: What supports your inspiration? What continually encourages? Praise, achievement, companionship, success, or seeing a difference in people's lives?

10 – The seeker.
Pathworking: In a forest clearing you meet a seeker. Perhaps personified by a grail knight, crusader, pilgrim, student or celtic seeker. You share your stories together. In his/her story he or she does not name that which they seek. Whenever they come close, you perceive the sparkle of love in their eyes. Then he or she asks you: "What are you seeking?"

11 – Ivy (Gort).
Sweet green ivy,
Curtaining my house.
You peep in at the windows
And comfort man and mouse.
You wind your flexy way
Sturdily up the tree,
Cuddling and caressing,
Yet letting it sway free.

12 – Roadkill
Meditation: At the site of a roadkill, an animal lies battered on the tarmac road. Travellers drive past. Some ignore and look hastily away. Some stare with gory fascination. Some turn heads to hide tears. A tiny few say a prayer, honouring the passing of the spirit instead of addressing the torn meat.

"Roadkill, Blood spill.
Spirit free, Blessed be."
- Chris Turner

13 – Play
Meditate on the value of play and theatricals, how they free you to be your inner self, and unlock the door to secrets.

14 – Praise
Write down all the good things you've done recently, caring moments and successes. Compose a poem to your own honour.

15 – Maidens of life
The Cauldron of Life, once sought by King Arthur, is tended by nine maidens, who heat the brew with their breath. In your life, what is the mixture inside? Which talents personified heat your life with their warmth?

16 – Monk
Pathworking: As you relax in your sacred inner place, you meet a wandering monk. He looks neither Buddhist or Christian. After greeting him, you question him. He tells you he is a Hunter Monk, that he is skimming and hunting in all religions for that which is full of Spirit. He tells you that there is a little Hunter Monk in each of us, someone who is hunting the truth of their soul. He asks you what you have learned from other religions and cultures, and how you honour them.

17 – Hedgehog. (Draenog)
Draenog, sweetheart, what a curious creature you are. Covered in spines and lifelong flees, you snuffle along in the leaves. Teach me that the most unusual amongst us need sometimes to use their ingenuity to practice unusual defense methods.

18 – Needs
Own your own needs. Instead of thinking yourself bad and selfish, acknowledge truth, do not deny yourself. If everyone is equal, you are a part of everyone, so pray or wish for something just for yourself.

19 – Starvation
Preservation methods have only recently enabled mankind to forget the importance of Harvest. In the days up to Harvest, food would have been scarce, as last year's preserved harvest began to dwindle. The last few days may have been without food. Ponder your times of spiritual starvation – when your spirit has been hungry. What preservation methods do you have to tide you from harvest to harvest?

20 – Fear
At this time of year, the Celts would have been awaiting the harvest, the fear of failure would have added momentum to their hard work. Meditate on fear and how it adds an edge to your inspiration.

21 – Mabon, Alban Elfid, Last Harvest
At this time of balance between night and day, meditate on the balance between harvested grain and spring-sown seed.

22 – Joy
Joy is a potent source of happy inspiration. What are the most joyous times in your life? Were they rites of passage or ordinary days? Where they special because of place, company, success or beauty?

23 – Terror
Not everything in life is fluffy and cosy and friendly. As a balanced human being we should not disregard the bad side of life. One bad side is the emotion of Terror. Spend some time thinking about terror and when it occurs. Finally, thank the spirits or your god(s) for the emotion of terror, which alerts you to danger and prepares you for taking flight.

24 – Ancient monuments
Which of the ancient sites inspire you the most? Stonehenge, Avebury, Glastonbury, Uffington, Callanish, New Grange, or somewhere else?

25 – Glittery eyes.
Pathworking – An ancient bard approaches you as you sit besides a wishing well. He carries a small harp and a flute sticks out a pocket in the folds of his clothes. His eyes are sparkly and glittering. You are drawn into their depths. Inside you can see the reflection of the stars, and the moon. You can see the play of sunshine on the ocean waves. The bard winks at you and is gone.

26 – Robes
Robes are not an essential part of druidry, but a tool used to focus, like wearing a business suit to work. Many druids get the idea for their robe during dreams or meditations, when their attention is brought to a specific design or fabric. Go for a walking meditation or inner one, to a material shop, and seek inspiration.

27 – Insects
It is easy to forget the insects in favour of mammals and birds, but they have many lessons. Meditate on butterfly, ant, spider, bee and ladybird.

28 – Reaping
Meditate and give thanks for what you have harvested this year

29 – The Sacred Land
Remember the times you have visited places of great beauty or power – landscapes of awe and sacred sites. Remember your closeness to deity and the Spirit. Take inspiration from your memories.

30 – The Oral Tradition
Why did the druids forbid learning from books? How does a religion or spirituality change without written doctrine? What is the advantage? How does it help you personally? Give thanks that your relationship with spirit is new every minute.

October

1 – Boar (Bacrie). The worthy adversary.
Meditation: Arthur, in the middle of the hunt for the boar Twrch Trwyth, pauses and speaks to his companions. He is weary. The boar is fast and ferocious, with fearsome tusks. Imagine his praise for the cunning boar, a worthy adversary. He speaks of the boar's strength and great stamina to match his own.

2 – The Moon
Meditate on the moon, and compose a poem to her beauty.

3 – Hibernation
At the time of cold, when heat departs and leaves anxiety, some animals find a way out. During your meditation today, hibernate, withdraw, relax and recuperate.

4 – Spontaneity
Active meditation. Today, be creative (a poem, music, drawing, craft, story, anything) without studying the subject. Allow your inner spirit to communicate without the bonds of other's opinions. Trust yourself and be spontaneous.

5 – Autumn
What are the treasures of autumn?

6 – Smell
Meditate on the many different smells and their messages and meanings. Start with grass, bread, seashore, mud and hot feet.

7 – Gold.
Pathworking: You are sitting on a sandy beach, with the sun blazing down, shining from the waters. Your skin is warm and glistening from the warmth. Besides you is a small pile of golden trinkets, charms and coins, which you run your hands through. You reach over and choose an apple or pineapple from a pile of golden fruit. You take a slice with a golden knife and bite deep. The flesh is sweet, and golden juice runs down your chin. What lesson is gold speaking to you today?

8 – Symbol
If you were a colour, what would you be? If you were a tree, what would you be? What if you were a bird, animal, feeling, tool, or song?

9 – Daydream
Wishful thinking and daydreams can be very inspiring. Have a good daydream about the past or future, and reap the rewards in the present.

10 – Leaves
Mini calendars of the year, this month they're unavoidable. Meditate on the Tree and the leaves as symbols of the season.

Bright green buds, unfolding to wide leaves full of the character of the tree, and now browning, turning orange, and beginning to fall.

11 – Druid Style

As Samhain approaches, in this time of reflection, consider the written style of these meditations and the similarities and differences to your style. For example, the importance of myth, deity, ancestors, nature and family rituals differ from person to person.

12 – Ellie

Dear Ellie,

I was thinking about you today as I read about Rhiannon in the Mabinogion. Her son was snatched from her, but no-one believed her and she was punished for his murder. In the event, he was restored to her years later, and in the meantime, she bore her punishment with majesty and courage. As the patron goddess of mothers separated from their children, I prayed she would give you courage as you wait to be reunited with your daughter overseas. Even physical death can't separate us from our loved ones. It's just a transition from one world to another. One day we will both be reunited with our daughters.

With love

Sandy

13 – Mistletoe

A special herb for druids, according to the Roman, Pliny, and others since. What do you think about Mistletoe and its associations?

14 – Shamanism

How easy do you find the Ovate part of Druidry, walking between the worlds, searching for a muse, divination, and communicating with spirits?

15 – Reed (Ngetal). Natural music.
Pathworking – you are walking besides a lake, and at the edge grows a bed of reeds. The wind is blowing through them, making them sway, swoosh, ripple and whistle.

16 – The crane.
Magnificent crane, with beautiful black white and red plumage. I thank you for reminding me of the moon in all her three stages.

17 – The ancient druids.
They were the ancestors of contemporary druids. We will never know exactly what they did and how they lived. Does it matter? Has the old knowledge been passed down despite their demise? Or are modern druids perverts of the beautiful ancient truths? Spend some time speaking to the spirits of the ancient druids, asking them for their blessing on your life and the way you live it.

18 – The Otherworld.
Many druids believe in existences of otherworlds, either under or over or parallel to this one. To meditate on the otherworld, you may feel safer viewing it through a picture frame, like the TV, rather than visiting as a pathworking, especially if this is your first time. Tune the TV frame into "Annwn", "Isle of Joy", "Sidh", "Tir na nOg", or simply "Otherworld". Watch the mists clear and a vision of the land appear. Similar to this one, only more sparkling, and of greater beauty. Watch for a while, and know that at any time you can simply switch the TV off.

19 – Mother Earth
Pathworking. In your sacred inner world, go for a nature walk through forests, meadows, by mountains, lakes, rivers, and deserts. Sail on the sea. It is a journey to meet Mother Earth. Greet her as a lady. Speak to her if you dare, or just observe. Watch the life that she supports. See the tiny people running busily over her tummy. Resolve to walk in a more sacred manner.

20 – Tor
Birth Mound.
Initiation. Divination.
Emergence from the Womb.

Smooth soft slopes,
Earth rising to greet the sky
In an untamed horizon.

Manmade breasts,
Where the lazy dragon
Winds its stealthy coils.

Death Chamber.
Dark. Muddy.
Land of the Fairies.

21 – The One Source
Meditate on old superstitions, old wives tales, folk lore and
witches herbalism in Britain, together with ancient civilizations
that seemed to know a lot of magic or hold strange beliefs that
are finally shown to be true. Co-incidence that such barbarians
knew science? Were the Egyptians, Celts, and Mayans trying to
teach their descendants? Or an affirmation that everything is
related, springing from the Gods, and that wisdom is given to
those that seek.

22 – Squirrel.
O gentle squirrel, bouncing tail, bounding through the forest.
Teach me your ways of preparing for the winter without a heavy
heart. Teach me to sniff out that which will sustain me through
the darkest hours. Allow me to follow in your springy footsteps
and curl into your soft tail, safe in the knowledge I can provide
for my own.

23 – Thunder and lightning
What a marvellous natural spectacle are thunder and lightning!
The prickle of electricity, and the build up to thunderous crashes
and glorious illuminations! What unnatural decorations can
compare to such inspiration?

24 – Quarters
What do north, east, south and west mean to you, individually
and together as a group?

25 – Mastery of Nature
The farmer attempts to master the land, sowing single crops in
one field and boxing animals in pens. The hunter-gatherer left
the land alone – a meadow with twenty varieties of herbs could
give fifty remedies and ten tasty dinners. Is there a
compromise, such as allowing animals freedom and benefiting
from their manure as they graze? What do you think?

26 – Magic Circle
Initially a scary, occult idea, a magic circle for a druid is simply a
place of blessedness, an area where your guests can be spirits
and gods. A special place. Create a special place for yourself
before meditations and note differences. If you find a balanced
circle too arcane, start with an irregular shape or sit on a sacred
mat.

27 – Year
As the Celtic year comes to an end, draw a graph or picture to
represent the last 12 months.

28 – Madness
What is the maddest thing you've ever done? What was the
most inspired? What do you see the difference between
insanity and feeling 'mad'?

29 – Life was harsher

Life was harsher
When rationing was in force
Make do and mend
Because our family is ruined
And half my family is gone

Life was harsher
With the coming of the cold time
The village elders say
"The wolves are running"
And half our flock is gone

Life was harsher
Before I knew you my lady
Embattled with uncertainty
And empty existence
Yes, life was harsher

© Jamie Wiseman

30 – Ancestors of blood.
Close your eyes and meditate inwards, to your DNA and physical make-up. Ponder your ancestors of blood, those who gave you that DNA, what they must have been like. Extend your respect to them.

31 – Samhain, Nos Calan Gaeaf, Meat Harvest
On this strange day between one year and the next, contemplate the stillness as the eye of the storm.

November

1 –Predecessors
Call to mind the most recently dead of your family. If you knew them personally, remember their ways, stories and achievements. Tell someone about them and keep their memory alive.

2 – Twilight
In the summer, a respite from hot days. In the winter, a warning time for preparation for the night. A deep gentle breath taken before plunging into dark. What are you preparing for?

3 – Dusk animals
Badger and fox, snail and owl, bats, fish, deer. Dusk animals that avoid the midday bustle, we salute you. Sometimes we also long to escape and melt into the welcoming twilight.

4 – The silver birch. (Beith)
At the beginning of the new year, meditate on new starts, births and the cleansing of renewal.

5 – Fae
Naughty little fairies
Do you really exist?
Tickling, poking, tempting,
When will you desist?

Jumping in the bath water,
Tugging free the plug.
Heading for the kitchen
To swig the milk down – glug!

Looking at the light fitting,
String a potato masher through it!
It wasn't me, mummy,
Mr Nobody made me do it.

6 – Wading through fallen leaves
A great delight for children. Consider why.

7 – The Drum.
Pathworking: You enter a clearing in the forest, and a man is sitting there with a drum in his lap. He is beating a gentle rhythm. He motions to you to sit down and he passes you the drum. He teaches you to play the rhythm he was playing. The rhythm is one you can take home with you and play whenever you wish to return to the forest clearing.

8 – Our descendents.
If you have children, spend time daydreaming and mentally preparing yourself for the gifts you will leave them. If not, think about your other babies – career, projects, creations. Thank the spirits for the inspiration of the future.

9 – Shamanic/Ovate tools.
Experiment with drum, rattle, rainstick, bells, voice and other noise, to see which you prefer. Which works for you, opening the door to the Otherworld?

10 – "Let there be Peace"
This call, the beginning of a druid ritual, reminds us that druids were once the diplomats and peacemakers in wars. It is a call for others to honour the ritual. It is also a call to ourselves, to still ourselves, to prepare. For without peace, the voice of Spirit cannot be heard.

11- War and Peace
The first druids were not only peaceful diplomats. Consider the impact of the sight of an army surrounded by druids lifting their arms to the sky and pouring magical curses on the enemy, whilst the women, roused in fury, shrieked and waved firey torches, stirring the warriors. Today, consider these druids, and the power you hold in your life.

12 – Fatherhood
What is your life experience of fatherhood? How does it reflect how you feel about men, especially those in authority, and the gods?

13 – What is your secret desire?
Pathworking – you are climbing Yr Wydda, a high mountain in Wales. Each step is difficult, and sometimes you must feel between the rocks and heather for handgrips. Your heart is pounding in trepidation, because you know that at the peak is an object that represents your hearts desire. Spend some time climbing. When you reach the summit, you find the item. You may be surprised or you may already have a clear idea what it is. You pick it up and nurse it like a baby.

14 – Laughter of delight
When the Awen of Inspiration comes to you, do you react with ferverous bardism, seriousness, or laughter of wonder and delight?

15 – Truth
Y gwir yn erbyn y byd – Truth against the World. What truths do you hold on to in your life despite the pressures of modern society?

16 – The Grove Setting.
Today's Druids love to meet in natural groves, in sacred circles and at beautiful locations outdoors. Past Druids also taught their students in caves, and secluded dales. Which natural places are sacred to you?

17 Animal Guide
Of all the animals – real and mythic – which are you most drawn to? Which are drawn to you? Which do you enjoy because their nature is familiar to yours, and which are stark yet full of wise teachings?

18 – Bravery
In the bardic tale of Culhwch and Olwen, Culhwch requests the hand of Olwen, daughter of Ysbaddaden. Ysbaddaden names many quests and tasks for Culhwch, to which he always answers bravely "it's easy for me to get that, although you think it isn't." What part does bravery play in your life? Culhwch had his cousin, Arthur, to help him. Who can you call on for help?

19 – Owl (Cailleach).

Wide eyed owl, silent flyer.
Friend of old mother knowledge.
Moonbeam faced fear-screecher,
Catching mice for the tiny owlets.
Lover of night and secrets;
With talons of death
And beak for tearing.
Champion of the solitary
And November's fear-cry
As it awaits the midnight of life.
Owl - how do you navigate the black?
How can that night be tamed?
Will you tell me,
Silent sweet death?
Or will you keep quiet
For another nighttime?

20 – Falling leaves.
Dance on the fallen, slippy leaves! Squidge them underfoot and feel their whisper as they tumble. They have done their job and now return to the earth. Catch one before it touches the ground and treasure it.

21 – Companionship
Although many tasks of a druid can only be performed alone, there are some which are strengthened by companionship. Compare the spirit journeys and pathworkings to times of song and dance. A choir and dancing friends inject inspiration, courage and support.

22 – The Ovate
Which methods of divination and seership have you learnt? Runes, Tarot, Ogham, speaking direct with spirits, reading natural signs, seeking visions in crystals, mirrors? Have you paid enough attention to intuition today?

23 – The Cauldron.
Meditate on the cauldron of inspiration, healing and rebirth.

24 – Tenacity.
Draw an image that represents the level(s) of tenacity in your life.

25 – Dream
What is stopping you from searching out and following your dream?

26 – Knowledge
Thought: Bardic colleges existed in Scotland until C18th

27 – Night
Compose a short verse dedicated to the silkiness of night. Silky silky night, soft and flowing sky.

28 – The Velvet Sky
Although it is cold now, meditate on the sky as a large, black velvet bedspread. Think of it as a warm black cuddle blanket, thick and rich, and decorated with twinkling glitter stars.

Now the nights are longer than the days, there is greater opportunity to ponder the comforting night sky.

29 – The Unseen
Hail to my Gods
Hail to my ancestors of blood and spirit
Hail to the sacred spirits of this place.
Hail to the sky above,
> the earth beneath,
> and the sea around.
Hail to the little people who crown around -
And to the names of legend who sleep.
Remember me today, as I remember you.

30 – Learning
How do you think you will learn more in the future – theory or practice? Reading or feeling, doing or failing, watching or researching?

December

1 – Computers and flint arrowheads
Meditate on the amazing powers of humans, and how far humankind has come from its early days.

2 – The Rowan tree. Protection
Pathworking: In your mind's eye, imagine yourself under the spread and protection of a rowan. Look safely on that which you are protected from. Feel the gentle peace under the safe branches – hear bird song and see animals graze – whilst outside a storm brews or blows. Imagine finding an umbrella discarded there, alone. Picking it up, you realise it is a gift to you and that its canopy is decorated with protective rowan branches and leaves.

3 – Awen

Thought: "The Awen I sing, from the deep I bring it, A river while it flows, I know its extent, I know when it disappears, I know when it fills, I know when it overflows, I know when it shrinks, I know what base there is beneath the sea."

4 – Family

In 1900 my Ninny was born,
Cheerful and bright, one maytime morn.
Generosity and truth were her special way
None ignored what she had to say

Complemented soon by a steadfast man,
Stubborn and kind, along came my gran.
Throughout the war they held to each other
The ultimate force was always "Mother".

In the fifties, my mummy, forceful and wild.
Compared to her, the family was mild.
The seventies brought a sister for me
We all gathered round to hear our Ninny.

Truth, honour and justice, I stick like a leech,
Letting out warcrys when someone's in breach
In 1999, my ninny was gone,
Somehow with love, life carried on.

That same year, my son was born,
Sliced from my womb one winter morn.
But when I look at his eyes in the light
I can still my Ninny's flame burning bright.

5 – Counselling
"Fair Elphin, cease to lament," said Taliesin. "To despair will bring no advantage, no man sees what supports him." What counsel and support do your friends need?

6 – Peace
This Wintertime, what are your peaceful blessings? What do you have to smile about as you and your loved ones gather round a metaphorical winter hearth?

7 – Winter Beauty
What special gifts have you been given this Winter? The sight of snowfall, the chirp of a robin, patterns of ice on the window, a taste of mulled wine, the clean smell of rain? Write some down to give you future inspiration when everything seems dead.

8 – Death
What will your last words be? Is your Will ready? Will you fight or accept death? What would you like as your funeral?

9 – Thought
The great thing about Winter is that you're always able to see the Dawn.

10 – Silver Fir (Ailim).
Are you called to stand proud of the environment, or is it ok to blend into the seasons, wearing winter and summer coats?

11 – The music of the wind.
If you listen to the wind, it blows in natural arrhythmic gusts. Listen to the soothing sounds, whether soft or furious. Imagine you are caught in a sticky spider's web. Feel the music blowing the cobwebs from you, setting you free.

12 – A flickering flame.
If you can, light a candle, otherwise imagine. Watch the flame dancing in the dark, free and happy despite the coldness around it, despite its knowledge that its life is limited. Pass your hand above the flame and feel the warmth, the generosity of the flame.

13 – Smoke Gazing
Either using, again, a candle, or incense burning, try your hand at divination through smoke gazing. Wormwood and Sage are good herbs for this incense.

14 – Snow.
Just as the sun is sinking in the night of wintertime, nature gives us a magical white gift of fun and mystery. The land is transformed and attention brought gently to the pleasure of life.

15 – The winterborn child.
The Winter Solstice marks the change when days begin to slowly lengthen again, the sun returning to its heat. It is like a mythical child, born in the depths of worry and cold death, bringing new life, warmth and hope.

16 – Nearest Nature
Where is your nearest patch of nature – a garden, farm, park, sea or rivershore? Meditate on what other answers other readers might give.

17 – Horse. Speed.
In pre-industrial times, horses were a great power, giving speed and easing distance and burden. Meditate on a place without cars and tower blocks, and with horses saved for important times. Consider the effect on neighbourliness and on stress levels.

18 – The sunset
Meditate on the sunset and the beautiful colours that fill the sky at that time of day.

19 – The Staff
The staff is a balance between authority and elderly dependence – magic, power, wisdom and the symbolisms of a walking stick. What balances are there in your life?

20 –
Thought: The death of the sun – what would it really mean?

21 – Yule, Alban Arthan
Thought: Midnight

22 – Bear (Arth). Strength and stamina.
Bear hibernates through Winter, emerging in Spring to test the sun's strength.

23 – The Birth of the Child
In Christianity, a birth of a child heralds a change, the start of a new religion. Meditate on other beginnings, births and starts.

24 – Excitement
For many children, this is Christmas Eve, a night when they excitedly await Father Christmas. What excites you in your life? What stops you from sleeping or thinking straight? When did you last show excitement?

25 – Christmas Tree
A Christmas tree is a powerful symbol in many homes today. Honouring the tree with decorations is a family affair. Consider your own Christmas tree.

26 – Gods
Following the excesses of materialism lately, seek out some time to meditate on spirituality, and your goddess(es) and/or god(s). Reaffirm to them and to yourself that you are a spiritual being. Look for the spirituality behind the shallow materialism.

27 – Mistletoe
If possible, bring a sprig of mistletoe into the house. Meditate on it, its shape, smell, symbolisms and meanings. Remember how Druids harvested mistletoe when it grew on the oak, and remember the kiss tradition under this yuletide plant.

28 – Winter Reflections for the New Calendar Year
Pathworking: Immerse yourself in a safe outdoor setting, dotted with birds, animals, trees and plants as you wish. Equate the things you see with moments from the past year. For example, a strong oak sapling could indicate a new job, a rabbit could represent a spiritual encounter with Spirit of Rabbit. Softly and slowly allow snow to gently cover the scene, creating a symbolic New Year. Allow anything you wish to keep to shake free of the snow. Let your mind work carefully, unrestrained by time.

29 – Bareness
The trees are stripped naked. Is it fair that you shut yourself in your house, hiding from the cold?

30 – Night
It is a terribly cold night. Whilst you are pondering spiritual questions, someone is dying. A freezing homeless night, empty but for the twinkle of the frosty stars, as the sky snuffs out their life.

31 – Calendar
Thought: Ways to count time eg: years from birth of Christ. Was time always so linear? Our biorhythms and women's lunar cycles teach us time flow in waves, like light which supposedly travels in straight lines.

Contacts

The British Druid Order
PO Box 29
St Leonards on Sea
East Sussex
TN37 7YP
UK

The Order of Bards Ovates and Druids
PO Box 1333
Lewes
East Sussex
BN7 1DY
UK

Ar nDraiocht Fein (ADF)
c/o Raven's Cry Grove
859 N. Hollywood Way
Box 368
Burbank, CA 91505
USA

Henge of Keltria
PO Box 48369
Minneapolis, MN 55448-0369
USA

Imbas
1412 SW 102nd St PMB 139
Seattle,
WA 98146-3770
USA

Philip Shallcrass, A Druid Directory, published by the BDO lists all the working Druid orders and Groves in Britain.

About the Author

Sandy Wiseman (aka Talyfox) began to write spiritual meditations in 1991, as a Christian using meditation, fasting and prayer as a key to God's heart. Moving on, she led a group of young people in a weekly quest for spirit in daily life, and shared meditations in Celtic rituals. Sandy has been a Pagan and solitary folk witch since 1996. She runs a Wiccan training circle in Nottingham, and with her husband she leads Apple Grove, a Druid Grove affiliated with the British Druid Order. She was initiated as a Bard at the Gorsedd at Stonehenge and regularly writes about modern druidry for websites and magazines.